WEATHER

Maria Koran

EYEDISCOVER

EYEDISCOVER

Go to **www.eyediscover.com** and enter this book's unique code.

BOOK CODE

AVF93993

EYEDISCOVER brings you optic readalongs that support active learning.

Published by AV² by Weigl
350 5th Avenue, 59th Floor New York, NY 10118
Website: www.eyediscover.com

Library of Congress Cataloging-in-Publication Data available on request

ISBN 978-1-7911-0766-6 (hardcover)

Printed in Guangzhou, China
1 2 3 4 5 6 7 8 9 0 23 22 21 20 19

072019
121818

Project Coordinator: John Willis
Designer: Mandy Christiansen and Ana María Vidal

Weigl acknowledges Alamy, Getty Images, iStock, and Shutterstock as the primary image suppliers for this title.

EYEDISCOVER provides enriched content, optimized for tablet use, that supplements and complements this book. EYEDISCOVER books strive to create inspired learning and engage young minds in a total learning experience.

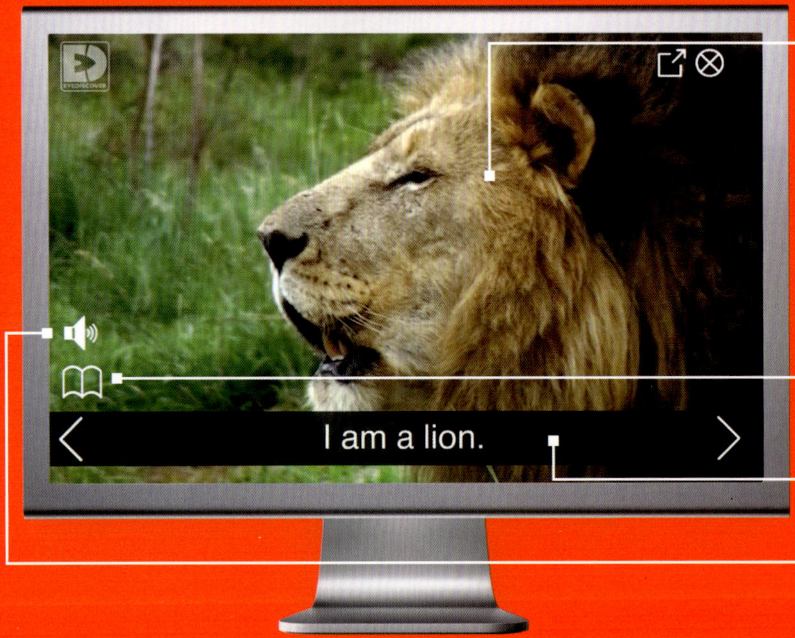

Watch
Video content brings each page to life.

Browse
Thumbnails make navigation simple.

Read
Follow along with text on the screen.

Listen
Hear each page read aloud.

Your EYEDISCOVER Optic Readalongs come alive with...

Audio
Listen to the entire book read aloud.

Video
High resolution videos turn each spread into an optic readalong.

OPTIMIZED FOR
- ✓ TABLETS
- ✓ WHITEBOARDS
- ✓ COMPUTERS
- ✓ AND MUCH MORE!

WEATHER

In this book, you will learn about

- what it is
- what it does
- how it works

and much more!

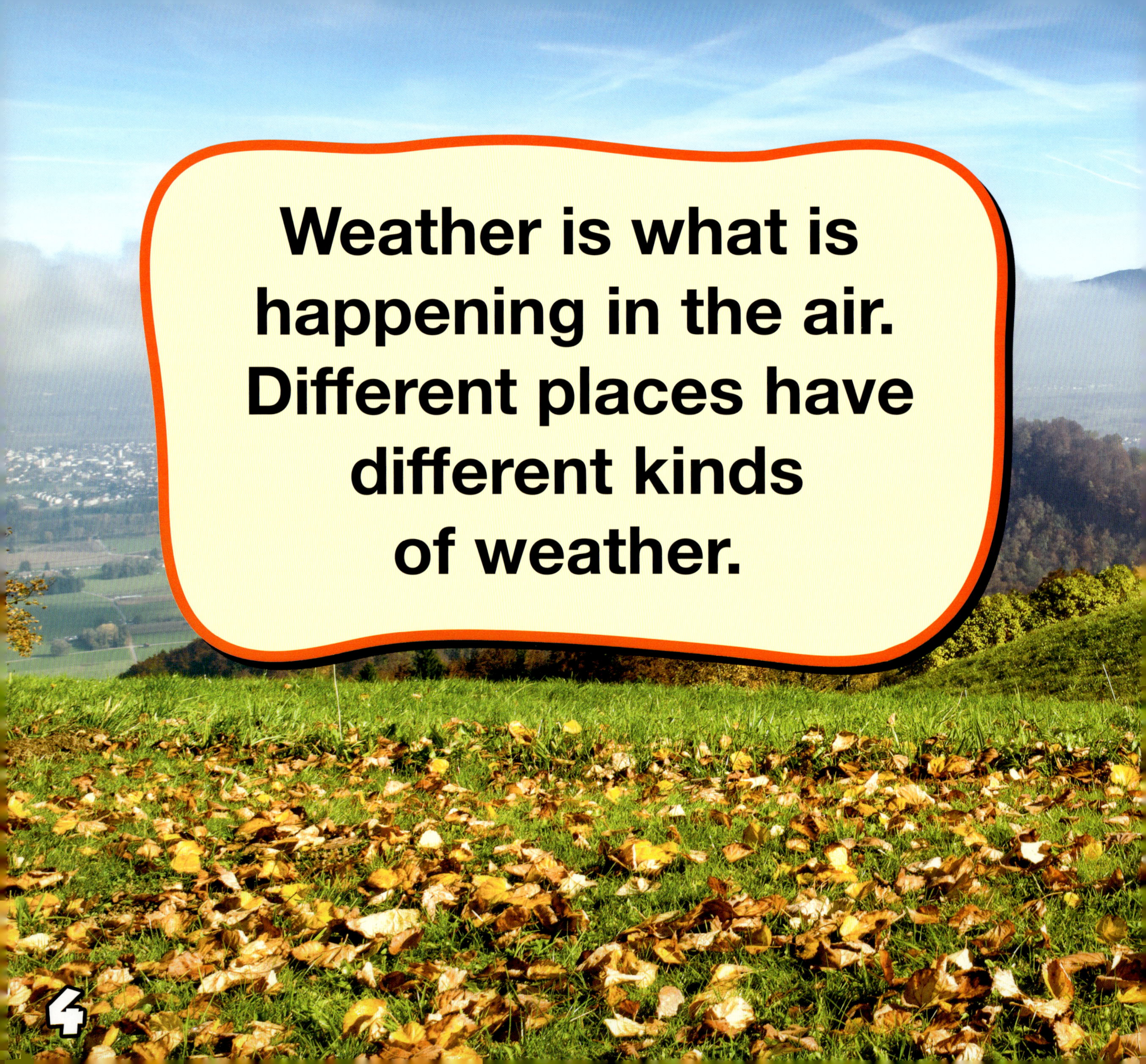

Weather is what is happening in the air. Different places have different kinds of weather.

6

There are many types of weather. Weather can be hot, cold, sunny, or cloudy.

Wind is made when air moves. People cannot see wind, but they can see how it moves things.

Clouds are made of water in the air. Clouds that are close to the ground are called fog.

Rain is when water falls from clouds. Rain helps give plants the water they need to live.

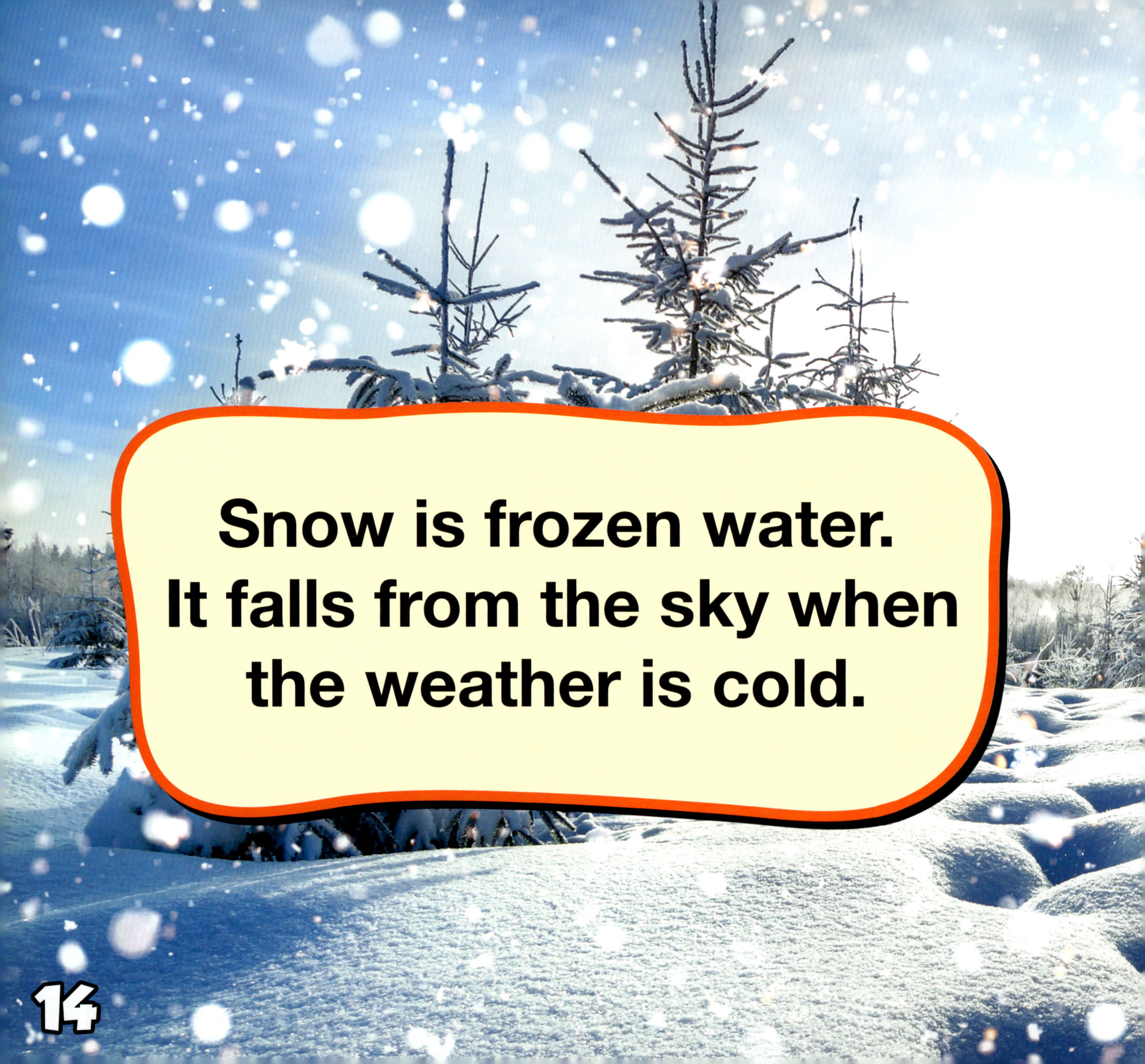

Snow is frozen water.
It falls from the sky when
the weather is cold.

Lightning often comes from thunderstorms. Lightning usually strikes high places.

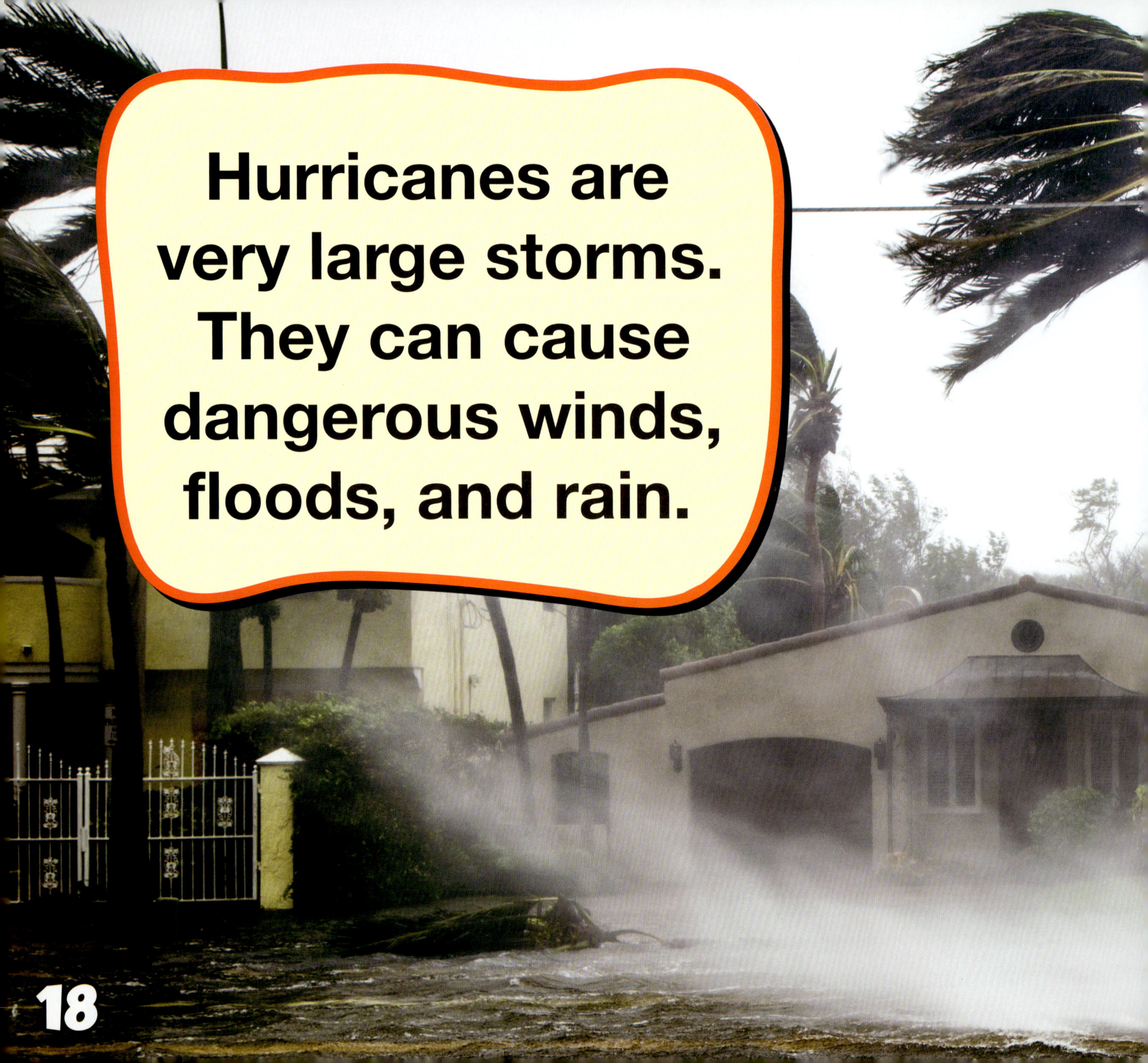

Hurricanes are very large storms. They can cause dangerous winds, floods, and rain.

Tornadoes are spinning tubes of air that touch the ground. They make the strongest winds on Earth.

WEATHER BY THE NUMBERS

The **highest clouds** are more than **20,000 feet** above **Earth.** (6,100 meters)

Most hurricanes are about **300 miles** wide. (482 kilometers)

All **snowflakes** have **six** sides or points.

There are **10 different** kinds of clouds.

The **United States** has more than **1,000 tornadoes** each year.

Lightning strikes Earth between **50 and 100** times every second.

KEY WORDS

Research has shown that as much as 65 percent of all written material published in English is made up of 300 words. These 300 words cannot be taught using pictures or learned by sounding them out. They must be recognized by sight. This book contains 44 common sight words to help young readers improve their reading fluency and comprehension. This book also teaches young readers several important content words, such as proper nouns. These words are paired with pictures to aid in learning and improve understanding.

Page	Sight Words First Appearance
4	air, different, in, is, kinds, of, places, the, what
7	are, be, can, many, or, there
8	but, how, it, made, moves, people, see, they, things, when
10	close, that, to, water
13	from, give, helps, live, need, plants
17	comes, high, often
18	and, large, very
21	Earth, make, on

Page	Content Words First Appearance
4	weather
8	wind
10	clouds, fog, ground
13	rain
14	sky, snow
17	lightning, thunderstorms
18	floods, hurricanes
21	tornadoes, tubes

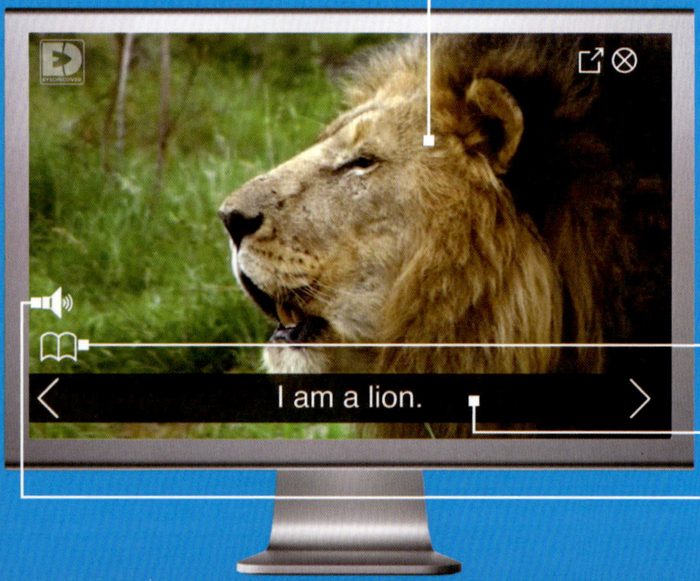

Watch
Video content brings each page to life.

Browse
Thumbnails make navigation simple.

Read
Follow along with text on the screen.

Listen
Hear each page read aloud.

EYEDISCOVER

Go to www.eyediscover.com and enter this book's unique code.

BOOK CODE

AVF93993